The Science of

Seasons

LIVING SCIENCE

Leslie Strudwick

Gareth Stevens Publishing
A WORLD ALMANAC EDUCATION GROUP COMPANY

Please visit our web site at: www.garethstevens.com
For a free color catalog describing Gareth Stevens' list of high-quality books and multimedia programs, call 1-800-542-2595 (USA) or 1-800-461-9120 (Canada).
Gareth Stevens Publishing's Fax: (414) 332-3567.

Library of Congress Cataloging-in-Publication Data

Strudwick, Leslie.
  The science of seasons / by Leslie Strudwick.
    p. cm. – (Living science)
  Includes index.
  ISBN 0-8368-2791-0 (lib. bdg.)
  1. Seasons–Juvenile literature. [1. Seasons.] I. Title. II. Living science (Milwaukee, Wis.)
  QB637.4 .S78   2001
  508.2–dc21
                                                    00-046386

This edition first published in 2001 by
Gareth Stevens Publishing
A World Almanac Education Group Company
330 West Olive Street, Suite 100
Milwaukee, WI 53212 USA

Project Co-ordinator: Jared Keen
Series Editor: Celeste Peters
Copy Editor: Heather Kissock
Design: Warren Clark
Cover Design: Terry Paulhus
Layout: Lucinda Cage
Gareth Stevens Editor: Jean B. Black

Every reasonable effort has been made to trace ownership and to obtain permission to reprint copyright material. The publishers would be pleased to have any errors or omissions brought to their attention so that they may be corrected in subsequent printings.

Photograph Credits:
Corel Corporation: cover, pages 4, 5, 6, 8, 9 top, 9 left, 9 center left, 9 right, 10 bottom right, 12 bottom right, 13, 14 center left, 15 top right, 17, 18, 20, 21, 22, 23, 24, 25, 26, 27 bottom, 30 right, 31; Digital Vision: pages 28, 29; PhotoDisc: pages 11 left, 14 bottom right, 15 bottom left; Tom Stack & Associates: page 27 center left; Monique de St. Croix: pages 9 center right, 11 right, 12 center left, 19; Visuals Unlimited: pages 10 center left (Bill Banaszewski), 16 (Sylvan H. Wittwer), 30 left (Albert J. Copeley).

Printed in the United States of America

1 2 3 4 5 6 7 8 9 05 04 03 02 01

Contents

What Do You Know about Seasons?

Many places throughout the world have four seasons in a year. These seasons are winter, spring, summer, and autumn. Does the place where you live have four seasons? Do you know which parts of the world do not have four seasons?

Each change of season brings new colors to the landscape.

In most of North America, each season has different weather. Winter is cold, summer is hot, and spring and autumn are in between.

The weather does not change on the day a new season begins. Instead, it changes slowly throughout each season. People feel the changes as each season comes and goes. Animals and plants feel the changes, too.

During winter, white snow blankets the ground where colorful flowers might have grown during summer.

Puzzler

Do you know which season it is now? Make a guess, then ask a parent or a teacher. Were you right?

What is your favorite season? What do you like best about that season? After you read this book, you will know more about seasons. You might change your mind about which season is your favorite!

Earth's Seasonal Cycle

Seasons change as Earth travels around the Sun. Earth is **tilted** on its path as it moves around the Sun, so Earth's North Pole and South Pole point toward the Sun at different times of the year.

Spring
Mid March to Mid June
Neither the North Pole nor the South Pole is pointed toward the Sun in spring. The weather is neither very hot nor very cold.

Summer
Mid June to Mid September
When the North Pole is tilted toward the Sun, the northern half of the world has summer. It receives the most light and heat from the Sun at this time. The weather can be very hot.

Winter
Mid December to Mid March
When the North Pole is tilted away from the Sun, the northern half of the world has winter. It receives little light and heat from the Sun at this time. The weather can be very cold.

Autumn
Mid September to Mid December
Just as in spring, neither the North Pole nor the South Pole points toward the Sun in autumn. The weather is usually mild.

It takes one full year for Earth to **orbit** the Sun. Winter, spring, summer, and autumn make one full year of seasons. Since Earth is always moving, the seasons are always changing.

Seasons in the North

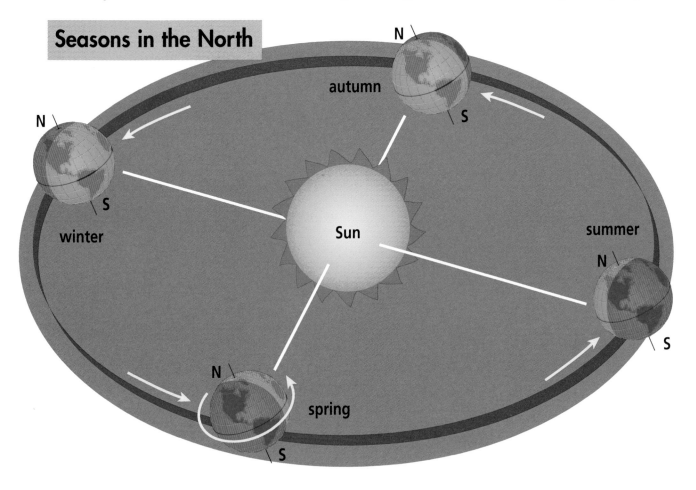

autumn

winter

Sun

summer

spring

Puzzler

When the South Pole is tilted toward the Sun, what season is it in Australia? If you need help, look at a map, a globe, or an atlas. See if Australia is closer to the North Pole or the South Pole.

Answer:
When the South Pole is tilted toward the Sun, it is summer in Australia.

Seasonal Signs

Each season has signs that go with it. When you think of a season, certain sights, smells, sounds, or ideas might come to mind. Some signs of Earth's four seasons are listed below.

Certain parts of the world have seasons like the ones on page 9. Can you guess where?

Seasons

Winter	Spring	Summer	Autumn

- cold temperatures
- snow and ice
- hibernating animals

- warming temperatures
- rain showers
- blooming flowers and budding trees

- hot temperatures
- green grass
- children playing outdoors and swimming

- cooling temperatures
- colorful falling leaves
- harvested crops

Puzzler

In which season do
many birds in the
north fly south?

Dry	Monsoon	Polar Winter	Polar Summer

Dry
- warm or hot temperatures
- lots of sunshine
- people on vacation

Monsoon
- hot, moist air
- strong winds
- heavy rain

Polar Winter
- extremely cold temperatures
- very long nights
- ground covered with snow

Polar Summer
- very cold temperatures
- very long days
- icy soil

Winter's Chill

December 21 marks the beginning of winter in the northern half of the world. This day is called the winter **solstice**. In winter, more hours of the day are dark than light. The winter solstice is the shortest day of the year.

In most places, winter is the coldest time of the year. It is a quiet season. Leaves no longer rustle. Few birds are left to sing. Insects have stopped chirping. Some animals sleep through the season. Their long sleep is called **hibernation**. They sleep until the weather is warm again.

When snow arrives, bears are ready for a long winter nap.

Trees do not grow during winter.

During winter, animals that eat grass and other plants have little food in places where the land is covered with snow. With little to eat in winter, animals usually eat a lot in autumn to help get through their winter hibernation.

People do not hibernate in winter, but they usually spend more time indoors. When people go outside, they dress for colder weather. They wear jackets, mittens, scarves, and hats. Even cold weather, however, can be fun! When snow falls, some people enjoy skiing down hills and along trails. When lakes and rivers freeze, some people go ice skating.

For many people, winter is a time to play in the snow.

Activity

Freezing Water

Do you have freezing temperatures where you live? To find out, try this experiment during winter months. Pour water into a paper cup until the cup is at least half full. Put the cup of water outside overnight. Does the water turn to ice? If it does, be sure to dress warmly!

Warm, healthy foods give people energy to get through winter.

Spring Has Sprung

The first day of spring in the north is near the end of March. This day is called the spring **equinox**. Equinox means "equal night." On this day, there are twelve hours of day and twelve hours of night.

Spring brings more warmth and light from the Sun, and Earth starts to wake up from its winter resting period. Many animals come out of their winter homes. Trees come to life again with their first tiny leaves. Grass that died in autumn is replaced by new green shoots. Wildflowers show off their beautiful blooms. Rain falls instead of snow. The Sun and the rain help plants grow.

When spring arrives, trees bud and flowers bloom.

Fields come alive with spring colors, and the air is filled with fresh, spring smells.

During spring, people help nature along. They plant fields of crops, vegetable gardens, and flower beds. Once the frozen ground **thaws**, farmers plant crops that will grow into food. Other people grow food in gardens. They plant seeds that will grow into tomatoes, carrots, beans, or other fruits and vegetables. People also plant seeds that will grow into flowers. The flowers will bloom at different times all through summer.

Activity

Spring Celebration

Many countries have a festival called May Day to celebrate the beginning of spring. Ask a parent or a teacher to help you find more information about May Day. Find out which countries celebrate it. When did it start? What activities take place on May Day?

Spring is planting season. It is the time of year when crops and gardens sprout and grow.

Summer Fun

Summer is a favorite season for many people. In the north, it begins with the summer solstice on June 21. With more hours of sunlight than any other day, the summer solstice is the longest day of the year. Summer is the warmest season. In some places, the temperature can get very hot.

Crops, flowers, and other plants that sprouted in spring **flourish** in summer sunshine. Spiders and insects, such as bees and butterflies, are common sights. Animals that were born in spring are growing and learning to take care of themselves.

During summer, spiders come out to enjoy the long, sunny days.

Most people love summer. Relaxing in the sunshine feels good.

Warm, sunny summer weather brings people outdoors. Parks, lakes, and trails are packed with people. Going to the beach is a popular summer pastime. Long hikes, bike rides, and sports, such as baseball and tennis, are also popular activities.

People in cities might go to an outdoor cafe, take a walk in a park, or sit by a pool. Everyone tries to make the most of long summer days.

A picnic is a fun way to enjoy a sunny summer day.

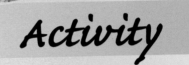

Activity

Fun with Bugs

Insects flourish in summer. Go outside and look around your yard for bugs and other tiny creatures. See how many you can find. Look under rocks, in the dirt, and near plants.

Try to find a worm, a spider, and a caterpillar. What other insects can you find? Maybe you can catch a firefly. Be sure to let the firefly go if you catch one!

Nature is full of life during the summer months.

Falling into Autumn

The lazy days of summer fun turn into crisp autumn school days near the end of September. The Sun rises later and sets earlier, and the temperature begins to cool down.

Autumn is a time for gathering food and preparing for winter. Farmers are busy harvesting their crops. Animals eat more and store food for the cold days ahead. Their fur starts to thicken, too. It will help keep them warm. Many birds fly south, or **migrate**, to a warmer place that still has plenty of food.

During autumn, people harvest food and get ready for the winter months.

Trees also prepare for cold weather. Some trees cannot **survive** winter without losing their leaves. The leaves collect snow and trap wind, causing a tree's branches to break. So, each autumn, these trees stop sending water to their leaves. As the leaves dry out, they change from green to red, orange, yellow, or brown. In strong autumn winds, the dry leaves fall off the trees and scatter over the ground.

Autumn is known for its colors. Green leaves turn red, yellow, and orange and flutter to the ground.

Puzzler

Autumn also has another name. What is it?

Answer:
Autumn is also called fall. This name refers to the leaves that fall from the trees.

Dry and Wet Seasons

Not all parts of the world have four seasons. Some places have only two seasons — a dry season and a wet, or rainy, season. These places are called the tropics. Because they are close to the **equator**, the tropics are barely affected by Earth's tilt. They face the Sun all year long, and the Sun rises and sets there at almost the same times every day.

When it is winter in North America, it is the dry season in the tropics. The weather is warm and sometimes hot. People from the north often take winter vacations in the tropics.

The tropics are warm throughout the dry season. People from cold places often travel there to escape the winter chill.

When it is summer in North America, it is the wet, or rainy, season in the tropics. Strong winds from the oceans bring heavy rain. In some parts of the tropics, the rain can fall for weeks at a time with few breaks. This time of heavy rain is called the **monsoon** season. When the Sun does come out, the weather is hot and **humid**.

Except during the dry season and the wet season, the weather changes very little in the tropics. Most days are warm and sunny.

During the wet season, the clouds open up. Rain can fall for weeks at a time!

Activity

Exploring the Tropics
Look at a map, a globe, or an atlas. Try to find countries that are in the tropics. Finding the equator first will help you. Most countries near the equator are tropical countries. Two examples of tropical countries are Brazil and Indonesia.

Polar Seasons

Two places on Earth have polar seasons — the North Pole and the South Pole. The areas around Earth's poles are cold all year. Temperatures might get warmer during summer months, but it is never hot.

In polar summer, the days are very long. Sometimes the Sun never sets. In polar winter, the nights are very long. Sometimes it is dark all twenty-four hours of the day.

Earth's polar regions are always covered with snow and ice — and the weather is always cold!

Living in polar regions is difficult. Very few animals can survive the constant cold, and not many people make their homes in these areas.

Some people live in areas just south of the northern polar region, even though it is still very cold there most of the year. Countries that reach into the northern polar region include Canada, Russia, and Greenland.

The Inuit are the Native people of the northern polar region.

Penguins live near the South Pole.

Puzzler

Can you name an animal that lives in both polar regions?

Answer:
Seals live in both polar regions, and some whales swim near both poles.

21

Seasonal Show-Offs

Some plants show us what time of year it is. Their appearance changes with the seasons. **Deciduous** trees are examples of these plants.

In spring, when the sunshine gets stronger and the temperature gets warmer, deciduous trees sprout buds on their branches. These buds turn into leaves. In summer, the hot Sun helps the leaves grow large and full. As the temperature cools in autumn, the leaves dry out, change color, and fall off. Rid of their leaves and standing bare, deciduous trees rest through winter.

The leaves of deciduous trees let us know which season it is.

Deciduous trees sprout new leaves every spring.

Most bushes and shrubs have the same growing cycle as deciduous trees. Many other plants change with the seasons, too. In cooler places, grass is brown in winter. In spring, it starts to grow again and turns green. In autumn, it stops growing and turns brown again. The bulbs of flowers such as tulips produce blooms in spring. Their green leaves soak up sunshine all summer, then fall off in autumn.

Flower bulbs and grasses are like deciduous trees. Every spring, they awaken to grow again.

Puzzler

What is the name for trees that stay green all year round?

Answer: Trees that stay green all year are called evergreen trees. Many evergreen trees are **coniferous.** They have needles instead of leaves, and they have cones. Pine trees are an example of coniferous trees.

Animals and the Seasons

Animals **adapt** to the seasons where they live. They must adapt to survive. Animals deal with changing seasons in many different ways.

Hares
in northern regions have fur that turns white in winter. Their white fur matches the snow, so they are not easily seen by **predators**.

Seals
have thick layers of blubber, or fat. Their fat keeps seals warm in the cold polar weather.

Woodchucks

hibernate through winter.
They eat large amounts of food in autumn to survive their winter sleep.

Squirrels

bury nuts and seeds in autumn.
They survive on stored food supplies until new food grows the following year.

Cats

shed a lot of hair in summer.
Having a thinner coat helps keep cats cool in hot weather.

Seasonal Work

Most people's jobs do not change with the seasons, but some do. Jobs such as fruit picking or snowplowing last only through certain seasons. A fruit picker can work only in summer or autumn, when the fruit is ripe. A snowplow driver works only in winter.

Some other jobs have duties that change with the seasons. Farming is an example. In spring, a farmer must **plow** the fields and plant crops.

Some farmers have huge fields of crops to care for through summer.

Plowing is usually done in spring or autumn.

The crops grow during summer. To protect growing crops from diseases or insects, a farmer might spray the crops with chemicals. If there is not much rain, a farmer must also water the crops.

Autumn is the busiest season for farmers. It is the time when farmers gather, or harvest, what they have grown. They store or sell what they harvest. Then, farmers prepare the land so it will be ready for planting the next spring.

Crops are harvested in autumn.

Activity

Do Your Own Research

Ask a parent or a teacher to help you research these seasonal jobs:

- fruit picker
- gardener
- landscape architect
- orchard owner
- ski lift operator

The autumn harvest provides farmers with food for winter.

Seasons in Danger

Temperatures on Earth are getting warmer. This warming might sound pleasant, but it is not. **Global** temperature changes can create problems. For example, the temperatures we now have during each season will change. Dangerous storms will happen more often. Some places will get too much rain, while others will get too little, making it difficult for farmers to grow enough food for everyone.

One cause of global warming is the gas, carbon dioxide. Although trees need carbon dioxide to live, humans are making too much of it. One of the ways people make carbon dioxide is by burning coal and oil. We burn coal and oil to produce energy and electricity.

Pollution affects the seasons. Too much pollution makes it harder for living things to grow.

You can help reduce carbon dioxide levels. Here are a few ways.

1. Do not use cups, dishes, or containers made of **styrene**. The chemicals that are used to make styrene increase global warming.
2. Plant trees and shrubs in yards and parks and on school grounds.
3. Reduce the amount of electricity you use in your home. Always turn off the lights when you leave a room.

Chemicals in the air cause global warming, but it can be prevented.

Seasons and Senses

The five senses are touch, taste, hearing, smell, and sight. People use these senses every day in every season. Look at the seasonal pictures on these two pages. How can you use your senses to enjoy these seasons?

Winter

Spring

Summer

Autumn

Answers:
Here are some ways in which your senses can help you enjoy the seasons. Can you think of any more?

Winter:
Watch snowflakes fall from the sky.
Catch them on your tongue and feel them melt.
Make a snowball and feel the icy chill.

Spring:
Smell some flowers.
Touch their soft petals.
See the brilliant colors of their blossoms.

Summer:
Watch ocean waves hitting the seashore.
Hear the roar of the ocean's surf.
Smell the salty seawater.

Autumn:
Watch colored leaves fall from the trees.
Walk through the leaves and hear them crunch under your feet.
Smell leaves being burned and hear the crackle of the fire.

Glossary

adapt: change to fit the surroundings.
coniferous: having needles and cones and staying green all year.
deciduous: shedding leaves each year.
equator: an imaginary line that divides Earth into northern and southern halves.
equinox: one of two days during the year when the hours of daylight and darkness are equal.

flourish: grow well.
global: all over the world.
hibernation: a long period of deep sleep during the winter season.
humid: full of moisture.
migrate: move to a place that is warmer and has a good food supply.
monsoon: a strong wind that brings heavy rain.
orbit: move around an object in a circular path.
plow: break up the ground for planting.

pollution: harmful wastes and poisons in air, water, or soil.
predators: animals that hunt and eat other animals.
solstice: the longest or shortest day of the year.
styrene: a foamy plastic commonly called Styrofoam®.
survive: continue to live, or exist.
thaws: becomes unfrozen.
tilted: at an angle.

Index

Web Sites

explorezone.com/earth/seasons.htm

www.epa.gov/globalwarming/kids/index.html

www.pghkids.com/Articles/Hibernation/Hibernation.html

Some web sites stay current longer than others. For further web sites, use your search engines to locate the following topics: *equinox, global warming, hibernation, seasons, solstice,* and *weather.*